D1172041

21st Century Skills Library

COOL SCIENCE CAREERS

SOUND ENGINEER

Patricia Hynes

Cherry Lake Publishing
Ann Arbor, Michigan

Published in the United States of America by Cherry Lake Publishing
Ann Arbor, MI
www.cherrylakepublishing.com

Photo Credits: Page 10, © Bettmann/Corbis; Page 13, © Mosaic Images/Corbis;
Page 19, © New York World-Telegram and the Sun Newspaper Photograph Collection
(Library of Congress); Page 20, © Dennis Galante/Corbis; Page 25, © Bettmann/Corbis

Library of Congress Cataloging-in-Publication Data
Hynes, Patricia Freeland.
  Sound engineer / by Patricia Freeland Hynes.
    p. cm. — (Cool science careers)
  Includes bibliographical references and index.
  ISBN-13: 978-1-60279-054-4 (hc : alk. paper)   978-1-60279-084-1 (pbk.)
  ISBN-10: 1-60279-054-X (hc : alk. paper)   1-60279-084-1 (pbk.)
  1. Sound—Recording and reproducing. 2. Sound—Equipment and supplies.
I. Title. II. Series.
  TK7881.4.H96 2007
  621.382'8—dc22   2007005701

Cherry Lake Publishing would like to acknowledge the work of
The Partnership for 21st Century Skills.
Please visit www.21stcenturyskills.org *for more information.*

TABLE OF CONTENTS

CHAPTER ONE

TOOLS OF THE TRADE

Good sound engineers have an aptitude for working with electric, electronic, and mechanical systems and equipment.

How would you like to be in the studio with your favorite musical group as they record their new album? How would you like to help that group make this recording their best ever? This is exactly what some sound engineers do.

The job of sound engineer involves knowledge

of science. However, it does not lead into the

laboratory, as many cool careers in science do.

Sound engineers help create what we hear at indoor

and outdoor concerts and on the radio, television,

compact discs, and movies. In this way, they make

use of both their scientific training and their ability

to use computer technology.

Life & Career Skills

What type of person might be interested in (and good at) this kind of job? Think of the key skills a sound engineer might need. Then, as you read this book, add to your description.

Sound engineers must be good at working as part of a team.

In this book, you'll learn what sound engineers do. You'll see the part

they play in making the finished product that you hear. You'll also explore

several jobs in the field. In the final chapter, you'll learn how a person

might train for such work.

First, let's look at the tools a sound engineer works with. The tools of a sound engineer include **microphones, speakers, recorders,** and **amplifiers.** At concerts, these are placed to bring the best possible sound to the audience. In the studio, these tools are used to get the best sound on record.

*Sound engineers must master a computer console
with dozens of dials to create the desired sound.*

A sound—a song, for example—can be recorded into a computer **console**. There it can be changed, just as we are able to edit our own writing on the computer.

Changes might include adding some more musical instruments. Or the artists and the engineer might "mix in" additional sounds. They may also change existing sounds to make new ones. These "tracks" can then be added to the one that holds the original song. This process continues until the artists feel they have brought out the music they have in their heads and put it in a form that everyone can hear.

CHAPTER TWO

MASTERS OF SOUND

Reel-to-reel tape recorders became popular in the 1960s and were replaced by digital recording in the late 1980s.

Less than 30 years ago, sounds were mixed using eight-track, reel-to-reel tape recorders. Each track was recorded. Then, the various tracks, such as vocals, strings, brass, and so on, were woven together. This was done

The Beatles and their innovative sound helped define music in the 1960s.

by playing the tapes all at once and recording them together. As you might imagine, this required an immense amount of time, patience, and skill.

Today's computers can do this in an instant, though they still must be controlled and guided by the musicians making the recording and, of course, by the sound engineer.

Albums of the classic rock group the Beatles were done this way. Their talent as musicians and songwriters was highlighted by the blending of many taped tracks. The music that resulted was a sound unlike anything that had been done before. These albums are also good illustrations of the collaboration, or working together, of the artists and the sound engineer.

Learning & Innovation Skills

Most of the old Beatles albums have been "remastered" and made available on compact disc or through music downloads like iTunes. Find out what *remastered* means. Why do you think some people like the sound produced by the older, reel-to-reel technology better? What can be done to make digital recording sound more "real"?

When he was in his early teens, Daniel Lanois set up a recording studio in his mother's laundry room. There he recorded local bands for about $6 a recording. What life skills was he exhibiting?

Sometimes that sound engineer is also a musician. This ability can add even more creativity to the process.

In pop music, French Canadian musician and sound engineer Daniel Lanois [lan-WAH] has won numerous awards. He writes and performs his own songs. His abilities, together with his vast knowledge of sound production, have allowed him to mix roles. He often plays instruments on the recordings that he works on as sound engineer.

Rudy Van Gelder was a favorite sound engineer for mid-century jazz greats such as Miles Davis, Thelonious Monk, and John Coltrane.

Learning & Innovation Skills

One of the important skills for a sound engineer is creativity. How was Rudy Van Gelder being creative in recording jazz artists?

In the world of jazz, the name Rudy Van Gelder brings to mind a different sort of sound engineer. Over the decades, Van Gelder recorded many jazz performers. His aim as a sound engineer was to produce recordings that were as balanced as possible—the kind of sound you'd experience if you were sitting in the best seat in a small jazz club. His efforts preserved the sounds of long-gone artists for generations to come.

CHAPTER THREE

POSSIBILITIES IN THE FIELD

Working in the field requires sound engineers to work quickly and efficiently in sometimes-difficult circumstances.

Not all jobs for sound engineers take them into the recording studio.

In fact, only a small percentage of sound engineers do work in recording

studios. Most jobs for sound engineers take them "into the field." This

means that the sound engineers have to go wherever the action is.

Music, Music, Music

One of the jobs for a sound engineer that many people know is to work on a concert tour for a rock band. Often these concerts are outdoors, and that fact can bring special problems. For example, what if a rainstorm delays the set-up of the *tons* of equipment? The sound engineer determines where to place the giant speakers and amplifiers. Then all the equipment needs to be wired together, which can mean *miles* of cables.

Once the equipment is set up, the sound check can begin. The sound engineer uses the computer console, a part of the band's touring equipment, to check sound levels. The engineer also uses the console to take out any

electronic whines, buzzes, or other noises produced by the equipment.

During the concert, the engineer makes sure the audience hears the best

sound possible. If the concert is being recorded, the engineer makes sure

that the recording progresses smoothly, too.

Sound equipment is fragile. Each piece is often packed in a separate box
that is very sturdy on the outside and padded on the inside.

If the band is on a world tour, the job of a sound engineer can be physically demanding, too. A tour means quickly setting up and taking down all the equipment, accounting for every piece, and boxing it to be moved. Then everything has to be set up in the new location. The sound engineer also may have to endure long plane rides, strange food, and time changes that literally turn day into night.

At War

Radio and TV news reports sometimes require sound engineers to work in the field, too. Obviously, a job like this is not for everyone. Sound engineers in the field have been killed or badly injured. Their

*Edward R. Murrow's famous radio broadcasts from London to millions
in America during World War II always began, "This is London."*

courage is beyond doubt. They helped bring us reports of World War II,

the Korean War, the Vietnam War, and the Persian Gulf War. They brought

us news of the invasions of Afghanistan in 2001 and Iraq in 2003.

Other News

Radio and TV reports cover a lot more than wars, and all the reports

need sound. There are press conferences, crime scenes, and accidents.

There are sporting events such as NASCAR races, the Olympics, and the Super Bowl. There are reports "on the scene" from the White House, the New York Stock Exchange, and political conventions. There are also interviews with politicians, actors, crime victims, and anyone else in the news.

At press conferences, sound engineers often have to position their microphones among others and still pick up what is said.

On movie and television sets, sound engineers set up special equipment to enhance, filter, or even change sounds.

Sound engineers are also critical to television shows that are made in the field. Think of all the home decorating shows. The sound engineers must record all the noise of demolition and construction. They must also carefully record all the directions on how to get the desired result!

Sound engineers also work in the field on animal shows. They must wade into swamps, climb mountains, and hang from trees to record both the animals and the people speaking about them.

CHAPTER FOUR

POSSIBILITIES IN THE STUDIO

If travel and danger are not in your plans, there are other sound engineering jobs that you might like. Many sound engineers do their work entirely in a **studio**. It may be a news studio. It may be a studio where weekly TV dramas and comedies are produced, or it may be a studio for soap operas, cable talk shows, or an early morning show.

Effective sound—and lighting—are two essentials for all TV shows.

The Evening News

Some sound engineers work on the Monday-through-Friday news shows from TV studios. As the program progresses, the engineer switches among commercials, live reports from the field, the studio anchors reading the news, and taped features. The engineer checks the console and adjusts sound levels for each segment. The job requires split-second timing, good physical coordination, and a great deal of knowledge about how the computer can help create the right sound.

Life & Career Skills

Sound engineers on news shows have to be very adaptable. They might be called to work on sudden notice. Why might this be true? Hint: Think of the explosion of the space shuttle in 2003.

The goal is for the sounds from all these different sources to go out to the audience clear and true. The engineer makes sure that listeners do not have to turn up the sound for one feature only to be blasted out of their seats by the next.

The engineer's console may take up most of the room in a soundproofed booth. Studio working conditions can range from posh to cramped. It all depends on the company the engineer works for.

At the Movies

Nobody worried about sound in the early days of movies. They didn't have any! Squeaky voices and loud coughs were not a problem. The dialogue was

*After "talkies" began, sound engineers even had to record
Metro-Goldwyn-Mayer's famous Leo the lion.*

printed on the screen. Nobody said anything. However, things changed

drastically in 1929 when "talkies" arrived. Ever since then, sound engineers

have also played key roles—offstage—on all movies.

Today's skilled sound engineers work hard to record the sounds of a movie. Then they make the movie's **soundtrack**. The engineer combines the voices of the actors, the sounds that are part of the action (sneezes, explosions, and so on), and the music. As he or she puts together these separate sound elements, the engineer must also constantly check the picture to be sure that the two agree. Attention to detail is a must.

CHAPTER FIVE

BECOME A SOUND ENGINEER

*Technology has become inexpensive enough for young people
to try out the career of sound engineer at home.*

As in most fields, there are personal characteristics that suggest an

aptitude, or inborn ability, for the work of sound engineer. Having a "good

ear" for sound is important. This is the ability to tell when something is

out of tune, for example. Learning to read music and playing instruments

can be helpful. Trying out music-making computer programs can provide a feel for what it might be like to do the real thing.

Anyone can twirl knobs on a computer console, but only trained sound engineers can do it with skill. Many employers expect training after high school to cover several areas. These include education in advanced electronics, sound production and transmission, broadcasting, and computer technology. After the formal education, it is possible to serve an **apprenticeship**. During this time, in return for lots of work and low pay, beginning sound engineers can get some on-the-job training from experts.

28

Learning what a computer console can and cannot do is essential to the sound engineer. Knowing how to get the desired results is essential, too. However, advances in the technology keep coming along. Interested students should try to keep up with these advances so that when they actually start their careers, they will be familiar with some of the tools. Being a little bit ahead of the game never hurt anyone!

Computers are here to stay in the work of a sound engineer, and staying up to date with the technological breakthroughs is important.

Glossary

amplifiers (AM-pluh-fahy-erz) devices that make sounds louder

apprenticeship (uh-PREN-tus-ship) job that requires working for a set amount of time in return for instruction

console (KAHN-sohl) panel of dials, levers, buttons, and switches that controls electronic equipment

microphones (MAHY-kruh-fohnz) instruments for magnifying sound electronically

recorders (ri-KOWR-derz) machines that store sound for later playing

speakers (SPEE-kerz) machines used to transmit, or send out, sound

soundtrack (SOUND-trak) recording of the music, voices, and other sounds for a movie, TV show, or other medium

studio (STOO-dee-oh) room or building where movies, TV shows, and radio programs are produced

FOR MORE INFORMATION

Books

Basta, Nicholas. *Opportunities in Engineering Careers.* Chicago: VGM Books, 2003.

Jones, Sarah. *Assistant Engineer Handbook: Gigs in the Recording Studio and Beyond.* New York: Schirmer Trade Books, 2004.

Maze, Stephanie. *I Want to Be an Engineer.* San Diego: Harcourt, 1999.

White, Ira. *Audio Made Easy (or How to Be a Sound Engineer Without Really Trying).* Milwaukee, WI: Hal Leonard Corporation, 1997.

Young, Clive. *Crank It Up—Live Sound Secrets of the Top Tour Engineers.* San Francisco: Backbeat Books, 2004.

Other Media

http://www.bls.gov/oco/ocos109.html is a federal government website that describes the job of a sound engineer in detail.

http://www.asee.org/ is the website for the American Society for Engineering Education, where you can learn about all sorts of engineering careers.

INDEX

ABOUT THE AUTHOR

Patricia Hynes grew up in Pennsylvania, where she climbed hills and trees and swam in the local river. She attended college in Pennsylvania and got a degree in literature and secondary education. In both high school and college, her writing was published in school literary journals. She has spent her adult life teaching and writing for young people and has lived in Baltimore, Boston, Chicago, Florida, and Canada. She now lives in Venice, California, with her husband, a painter and dentist, and a fluffy orange cat named Stinky.